My Sol to Keep

A Book of Poetry

DominiQ Smith

My Sol to Keep

A Book of Poetry

DominiQ Smith

Published by "DominiQ & Co."

Printed in the United States of America

U.S. Copyright © 2021 No. 1-10734322741

ISBN: 978-0-578-96347-1

Dedication

To my grandmother, my best
friend, my soul sister, the
brightest star in my sky.

I love you always.

Thank you for giving me art.

Lady in Blue

A woman dressed in blue, your heart
sings the saddest sorrows the world
ever knew, blue and borrowed and
someone bruised, bright red blood
drawn to your surface you are forged
through the fire that curls around
your lips Sunday dress that curves
around your hips.

The hips that bore children and pain.

You've raised up broken men,

your heart scarred by their sin,

you have moved mountains with your
hands and built cities with your
mouth.

A woman dressed in blue, you are blue
and borrowed and bruised, but you are
never broken,

woman in blue, you are free.

Free from every ache and every pain.

The sky is painted with your
presence, and your love is rain.

A woman dressed in blue,

your hands riddled with veins like a
map of your life

A display of all the broken roads
that lead you to paradise.

A woman whose love healed the broken
and bruised,

you taught me the most fervid flame
burns blue.

The Journey

I wrote this at a time in my life
where the world without my
grandmothers' presence seemed blue in
a way that made me burn with love and
rage all at once. I struggled to
process the thought that someone I
had grown so attached to was no
longer within reach. I had loved her
just as much as I was angry.

For a long time after she died, I was
at a crossroads with my anger. I
couldn't decipher what to be angrier
at or even if I had any right to be
angry at all.

I hated the fact that she was gone,
the fact that she finally had peace
even if it meant chaos for me. I

hated that I loved her so much that it hurt because, in the end, I had no choice in the matter. Who was I to be angry at her for dying? How selfish could I be!? It was a constant battle within myself. One that I felt like no one understood.

If I could've taken all of my emotions and tucked them away into a box, I would've. Yet I poured them onto paper, and I found peace.

As I wrote, I began to unravel different images of her in my mind. The silly woman I had always admired transformed into the fighter, the lover, a gift not only to me but to the world.

My whole life, I had gotten to experience her constant love and beauty, but I know now that so many others did too. I also understood that not everyone knew how special she was. Part of me ached at the thought of how under-appreciated she was. The same way that so many of us live our lives without giving the sun a second thought until were basking in the light of the moon, knowing that no other light compares.

This one is for the women, like my grandmother, who spend their life loving in an undeserving world without a second thought.

She was the mourning sun,

eager to serve a world plagued by
pain.

Much like the sun, which irrevocably warms the earth, she poured her love onto those who needed it most, and I genuinely believe that was her purpose in life. I know that in the way that she prayed, her heart ached for people as if it were their own.

She never asked for anything. In return, all she wanted to do was spread love into the world, and everyone that she touched was affected by that. She was such a strong presence in so many people's lives I don't think that anyone would say she was less than incredible. To say that I was privileged to know that I had this amazing connection with somebody so beautiful is an understatement.

Nothing can express the amount of gratitude I have for what we shared. She was exceptional. She was the kind of woman that mended the broken people of the world. It was her desire and her life's goal to lead them in love. I think that is what made it so easy to love her. She deserved all of the love that she gave.

Her lipstick stained my soul the way
the sun burns your skin.

It left me on fire in the most
beautiful way.

She would kiss my face leaving the residue of her favorite red lipstick. As I grew into a woman in her image, the same lips that stain my cheeks red, they burned her words of wisdom into my soul and forged me at my core. Her words had the power to move mountains in me.

It was a beautiful experience to feel her presence. By no means was she a saint, and she would be the first one to tell you. Sometimes she was a little too honest and a little intense in complicated ways for some people to handle, but it was her love and honesty that I needed.

I had to feel the wrath of her love sometimes, in a way that made me uncomfortable so that I could grow.

I think that when somebody truly loves you, they push you beyond your comfort zone, they question your ability, and it creates a better version of you. Growing is never easy, but it is so much more rewarding when you have someone who encourages you to feel the rawness of growth. She planted seeds within me that I will grow for the rest of my life. For that, I am eternally grateful.

The unconditional, true love that she spoke into my life sparked everything good that I have ever become. She is every reason that I am.

She was like the summer sun on a
winter morning,

her warmth was enough to reach the
darkest, most frigid places in the
world

There are times in our lives when we will weather the winter storm. Lasting days and nights and sometimes weeks that seem like one big dark room. Despite the longevity of the hard times, she visits more frequently than the pain. She is always there to remind us that even on the coldest days, we can experience the sun.

I am also reminded by the thoughts that no matter how far the sun may be, sometimes its presence is strong enough to feel even thousands of miles away. Isn't it amazing that the sun can feed life into the seeds beneath the soil?

So much that they flourish into beautiful flowers. It is a kind reminder that no matter where our soulmates may wander, we may still be able to feel them. That is the hope that has given me momentum in my mourning.

Her light struck my windows pain,

In a room, I had abandoned long ago,

it was her light that gave me the
strength to grow

Losing her felt like the ground shook beneath me. There were so many unanswered questions in the history that she never spoke of. It felt like my life had been uprooted only to be planted in a place that was seemingly impossible to grow out of. In my cold dark room created by the walls of my grief, she made her way to the only opening I had left, and she brought me hope.

I went through a phase in my grief where I felt like a shell of a person, and I couldn't understand how the emptiness could serve me any purpose. I sunk into a depression that nobody could pull me out of.

Friends and family all spoke of the silver lining and the bright side of things that were nowhere to be found.

It made me furious because no one could see how empty I was. No one knew that there was no light in this room I had locked myself in. I had longed to escape myself. Yet I had all of this empty space, and I felt idle as if there was nowhere to go. Even worse, there was nowhere to hide.

I was forced to move through this life without her, and I felt lost. It wasn't until I recognized the bits and pieces of her in my everyday life that I found hope. I started to see her in the way I spoke, in the micro-stories of memories I had. She was at the center of so many of my inside jokes. It's like she existed everywhere and nowhere all at once. I was a mosaic made from memories of

her. It was that small beam of light
in my life that broke the darkness.

At first, it was just the amount I
needed to feel warm, and suddenly it
was the fire I craved to thrive.

You were the sun, and I became the
moon, haunted by your absence

I experienced days of eternity and nights drowning in my sorrow, longing for the morning to come so that I could experience a new day, a new beginning.

Even though I was terrified to experience a life in which she did not exist, living in the moment was agonizing. I wanted the pain to end. Still, a part of me didn't want to move on if it meant accepting that I had to live without her.

I felt like every day that I was living when she was not, I was being taunted by the universe. I felt like my pain was a cosmic joke. I just couldn't seem to understand. I spent countless nights under the moonlight, trying my hardest to appreciate it.

Just hoping that it would be enough.
Nothing was the same. Nothing lit me
on fire the way she did. I know that
I will never experience that again.
That is the hardest part of it all.

Eres mi sol, la pasión que arde en mi
vida

* you are my sun, the burning passion
in my life

Out of all of the things that she left me with, it was her passion for life for her love for art. That is what has been my light. It is what drives me through the darkness. I have the same passion that she had in her life, and it is how I have delivered myself from the pain.

Art brings us beauty in all things. Sometimes it was sweet poetry. Other times my heart sang in the shower through violent screams. I absolutely unapologetically had to release the pain inside to heal. I had to re-discover my passion for life.

It was an emotional journey that was unpredictable at times. I had to accept every day as if it were the first. Prepared to accept that some

days would be more challenging than
others.

I never experienced pain until I
watched myself die with the person I
loved,

That is what losing a soul mate is
like.

We experience soulmates in different forms and magnitudes, and it is a painfully unique experience whenever we lose them. There is no other loss that compares to losing a person. You have an indescribable connection in your life. When you lose your soulmate, you lose yourself.

There is an almost out-of-body experience that we go through when we grieve that kind of loss or a loss of that magnitude, and you can see yourself through the pain. However, I could see myself through the grief, but I had become so unrecognizable I felt like I had been locked out of my own body inside a prison of my mind. Surrounded by my thoughts with no way to control them.

So disconnected from my heart. When I lost her, it broke me in unimaginable ways. Now I was nothing more than a scattered mess compiled of mixed emotions and distant memories.

Only I had the power to find the pieces and put them back together. I knew that it would not be easy. They say that time heals all wounds, but time does not erase scars and trauma. So through time, I managed to bring myself back together, and I waited and waited for the pieces of me to mend together.

Nonetheless, I still had to live forever, altered by my pain. I will never be the same person before losing her. This new version of me is not better or worse; it's just missing the most crucial part.

It's a version of me that I am
learning to love every day. One that
I am sometimes unkind to.

We must remember, but it's important
to be gentle with ourselves, and even
though we may not have a perfect
track record with that, we should
always remind ourselves that we have
the right to take our time to grieve.

I watched the sunset in her, the
light slowly dwindling away,

leaving my world in darkness.

I stood by her in her last days, holding her hand that grew colder, watching her lie so peacefully so still. I couldn't help but feel like I was standing before a stranger. Not because she was unrecognizable but because I knew she was dying and her spirit was not the same.

She wasn't laughing or speaking; she was just still. She was never anyone that was still. She was filled with passion, momentum, and an unmatched amount of ambition. Now that she was no longer those things, and as I saw her fade into a memory, I felt like I was simultaneously losing myself.

Sometimes when we experience seeing our soulmates leave this world, we can feel the life escape from our bodies.

What I mean by escape is that as much as we try to hold onto that life, it's almost as if we are fighting against it to contain something that is unfortunately meant to leave us.

Eventually, when this happens, we Don't really experience anything other than the pain at that moment. Yet when we begin to heal ourselves and we look back, it's much easier to recognize the beauty in it all. I'm grateful that she wasn't suddenly ripped from me.

It is a bittersweet experience, like the sunset of a day that you never want to end. It may hurt to watch them go, but I am so content knowing that I got to hold her hand as she left this world. I understand this world was never good enough for her.

She was more than anyone ever deserved. So all of the pain that she had endured in her life it's finally gone. As much as I will miss her, I know that she is at peace.

She will never have to experience the pain that I have. If I had to endure losing her, so that she didn't have to endure losing me, that is a pain I'm willing to accept.

I'm reminded of her with the rising
of the sun. Her spirit brings life to
my day.

There isn't a day that goes by that the memory of her doesn't linger in every thought, every word spoken, in every action taken. She is the first thought in the morning and the last before bed end. It is that thought of her that takes me from sunrise to sunset.

I still have to remind myself to rise with the morning sun most days and give myself another chance. Every new day brings new challenges in this journey of grief. Some days I am warmed by the memories of her, and I feel at peace.

Other days I am scorched By the thought of her absence. Somehow even in a universe away, she found a way to keep me alive.

In all my grief, I had managed to find the strength to pull back the curtain and let the sunlight shine in. I remembered that it had never truly left.

My eyes, like my heart, had been shutting it out.

Sometimes we are so consumed by our grief that we allow it to blur our vision. It becomes hard to see what has been in front of us all along. And what seems like forever suddenly ends in a moment.

Just as we were broken all at once, we are also somehow suddenly okay. Not truly happy or wholesome, but just OK enough, finally pull back that curtain and Live again.

The hardest part is realizing that you become vulnerable again when you remove the callus from your heart. Allowing yourself to find peace after grief requires strength. For a long time after losing her, I allowed the grief to overpower me.

Finally, the tables had turned, and I was able to take control of my pain.

Not in a way that I could make it
disappear or ignore it but in a way
that I could grow from it. So that's
what I did. I gathered all the pain
within myself, and I turned it into
my strength.

I was sun-kissed, a few shades deeper
than love.

This one is for the mothers that we lose too far too early. The ones whose love created us in their wombs and hearts. Our skin is created in their image just a few shades deeper than their love.

We may not have them in our lives anymore, but may we have their skin, beauty, and flaws. May we be a mosaic of bits and pieces that they were. Because that is how we gather the strength to face our reflection again. We learn to love ourselves the way that they would have loved us. The way that we deserve to be loved. Unconditionally. Unapologetically.

What a beautiful disaster it is to find yourself in the loss of a loved one.

To find your roots in the midst of burying yourself.

To feel reborn through the grief that was meant to break you.

I realized that when I began to take myself into my mind full of thoughts of anger and pain that I had the power to find myself again.

As I lied in my sorrow, the sorrow that was my grave, I thought truly my life had begun to end. The crushing pain in my chest felt like I was taking my last breath. Then just as I lay still ready to succumb to the pain, and despair, prepared to die, I discovered a new reason to live.

Like a buried treasure, I emerged from the soil, weathered and worn but still so valuable. I was forever changed, but nothing less. I wasn't meant to live without you, and that is why it hurts so much.

Even so, I will continue to live for you. I will be all that you would've wanted and more.

Here you are after all the pain and suffering.

Today you woke up, today you won.

Often grief can feel like a war within us. When we tell ourselves that everything happens for a reason or that they're in a better place, but our heart knows that the pain is too real to reason with.

When your mind and your heart are trying to move in different directions, It can feel like you're being torn from the inside out. There are some of us that experience this without ever saying a word.

We go through life waiting for it and almost hoping that it would just end. We don't realize at the moment that every day we wake up, we are winning. Every day we conquer our pain by enduring it.

So remember that when you wake up each day, even if it hurts, even if

you have to fight, even if it feels
impossible, you WON. War heroes never
emerge from the war unscathed.

Take your battle wounds and be proud.
You deserve it.

I've learned to give myself the love
that I had longed to give you since
you left,

That is when I was able to heal
myself.

I felt like I would never feel the kind of love I had felt from her. I searched for that kind of love in empty people and shallow places. But when I was able to understand that the love I have been searching for was the one that she had taught me, that's when I was able to give it to myself.

The best part of being so inner-twined with someone is understanding their perspective. I think she was the only one who ever truly could see through me who could hear me without ever speaking. Yes, still, she loved me.

I thought that if I was worthy of being loved by such an amazing creation, I should still be worthy of love.

So I took the love that I knew she would've given me, and I used it to mend all shattered pieces of my heart.

Perhaps in some ways, it was her plan all along. Maybe she knew there was an end. Perhaps that is why she built me up so strong. If so, then I am even more grateful than before.

I finally overcame the emptiness that
consumed me when I understood it was
the space I needed to grow.

My life Was so full of love and happiness before I lost her. I was so content with the life that I had. So complacent. When she was no longer there, I felt empty. For a long time, I had thought that there was no purpose to this pain.

I could not see any reason to feel so empty. When I did not realize is that growth is sometimes painful. There was now a hole in my heart forever. Slowly but surely, I begin to fill the void with patience and kindness for myself.

The way that I know she would've wanted me to. I took the seeds Of strength that she had left me, and I grew a garden of love. The grief that I had once felt made me regret loving somebody so much.

Maybe if I hadn't loved her the way I did, I wouldn't have hurt as much losing her. The most important lesson I have learned through my healing is that even though we grieve our loss, we can celebrate our love.

I shed the weight on my chest with the tears from my eyes. I learned that I had to embrace the grief to overcome it. I had to accept the pain or be consumed by it. There were so many moments that I had tried to hold back the tears to keep myself together for the sake of appearance. I wanted so much just to be okay that I felt like I could pretend enough that eventually I would be.

I found peace in my cries.

Thank you for keeping me warm all
these years,

Thank you for the light and the life
you gave,

Thank you for being the gravity I
needed while my life spun out of
control

You are my sun. You are my sol to
keep.

I often reflect on my relationship with you, and I'm grateful for the experience. Even if it ended so abruptly, I was given the most beautiful time that we shared. I am grateful for all of the times that you were my security and sanctuary.

As I navigate through life and some of the most challenging times of my life, it seems like you were always there to bring me back to my center, not in a way that held me back but in a way that grounded me.

Losing you seemed like I had lost the gravity. It made me feel like I was lost in space. I know now more than ever how much you truly meant to me.

I am sure that you were my sun and you forever will be my soulmate.

Soulmates come in many different
forms sometimes.

Sometimes we have one, sometimes we
have many, and wherever life takes
me, whoever I cross, I will have
lived a life where I know, but I have
found at least one of my soulmates.

I will cherish that forever, and hold
on the memory because you are my soul
to keep.

About my Grandmother

This book was written and dedicated
to my late grandmother, who was
someone I was deeply connected with
in a way that I had never connected
with anybody else. I felt every ounce
of joy leave my body when she died.
The pain that sank into my stomach
has lingered ever since.

I have tried to process the thought
of her being gone, and it has been
seemingly impossible at times, but
the one thing that has got me through
is poetry. My grandmother was a
strong woman but a passionate one.
She taught me so many forms of art,
and it was her livelihood.

She was a mother, a wife, a friend, a
sister, a partner, a preacher.

Above all, she was a lover. She loved the world like no other, without hesitation, and unconditionally. Her love was something I aspire to have because I understood the way that she loved.

I understood her on a level that I believe only soulmates can understand one another. I could feel her presence throughout my whole life until the day that she left, and that's when I knew that losing her would leave my world in darkness. My grandmother started a legacy with her love. Everyone she touched created a ripple effect.

There's not a single person that I have spoken to that can say she was anything less and light itself. She was bright and beautiful and sometimes so intense that she was blinding. She was too much to handle for some people, but she was everything they needed for most. She had a sharp tongue sometimes, and she was too opinionated sometimes, but she never failed at anything.

I will never forget how I spent summers with my grandmother, bonding over tea parties and breakfast on Sundays. I have memories of going to church with her and doing arts and crafts in her kitchen all summer long.

I hold on to those memories, hoping her love is reflected through this book. So the memory of her love continues to shed light.

For the people navigating through the dark times, I pray that you see the sun again.

Contact

For bulk purchases, comments, or questions you may have, please email me at:

dominiq.castanon@yahoo.com

www.ingramcontent.com/pod-product-compliance
Lightning Source LLC
LaVergne TN
LVHW021615080426
835510LV00019B/2588